READY SET STAAR

FOR TEXAS
SCIENCE SUCCESS

NATIONAL
GEOGRAPHIC

School Publishing

PROGRAM CONSULTANTS

Randy Bell, Ph.D.

Kathy Cabe Trundle, Ph.D.

Judith S. Lederman, Ph.D.

David W. Moore, Ph.D.

Grade **4**

REPORTING CATEGORY 1
MATTER AND ENERGY

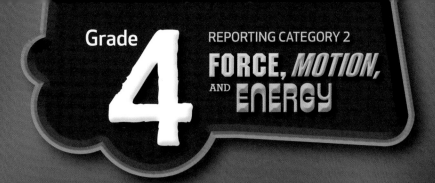

Grade 4

REPORTING CATEGORY 2

FORCE, *MOTION,* AND ENERGY

PAGE 28

PAGE 32

PAGE 36

Dall
Austin

PAGE 46

PAGE 50

PAGE 58

PAGE 70

PAGE 72

Grade 4

PAGE 78

PAGE 82

Lancaster Sound in Nunavut, Canada, is located in the Arctic. During the spring, the Sun shines for up to 24 hours a day. Energy from the sunlight warms Earth and starts to melt the ice. In late August, the days get shorter again. The temperatures become colder. Ice covers the area for about nine months a year.

MATTER AND ENERGY

REPORTING CATEGORY 1: MATTER AND ENERGY

The student will demonstrate an understanding of the properties of matter and energy and their interactions.

3.5 MATTER and ENERGY
The student knows that matter has measurable physical properties and those properties determine how matter is classified, changed, and used.

STATES OF MATTER

Take a close look at the photo. What do you see? You see **matter!** Everything around you is made of matter. Matter can have different forms. These forms are called the **states of matter.** The states of matter include solid, liquid, and gas.

voCAB

matter
(MA-ter)

Matter is anything that has mass and takes up space.

states of matter
(STĀTS UV MA-ter)

States of matter are the forms in which a material can exist.

SUPPORTING STANDARD TEKS 3.5.C:
Predict, observe, and record changes in the
state of matter caused by heating or cooling.

Solids have a definite shape. A rock and a block of wood are examples of solids. Liquids, such as water in a bottle, take the shape of their containers. The air is made up of gases. Gases spread out to completely fill a space.

The boat is a solid. The water in the ocean is a liquid. Air is a gas. Moving air, or wind, can push objects, like this sail.

My science notebook **WRAP IT UP!**

1. **Recall** Describe three states of matter.

2. **Contrast** How are liquids and gases different?

3. **Apply** Is honey a solid, liquid, or gas? How do you know?

5

INVESTIGATE
FREEZING AND
MELTING

 How do cooling and heating affect different liquids?

Matter can change state when the temperature changes. In this investigation, you can observe what happens when different liquids are cooled and heated.

MATERIALS

2 plastic cups   **graduated cylinder**   **water**   **salt water**   **tape**   **2 thermometers**

SUPPORTING STANDARD TEKS 3.5.C:
Predict, observe, and record changes in the state of matter caused by heating or cooling.

1 Use a graduated cylinder to measure 50 mL of water. Pour the water into a cup. Label the cup. Repeat with salt water.

Water

2 Put a thermometer in each cup. Measure the temperature of each liquid and observe its properties. Record your data in your science notebook.

My science notebook

Salt water

3 Put the cups with the thermometers in a freezer. Predict what will happen to the liquids in the cups. Record your predictions. The next day, take the cups out of the freezer. Observe the properties and record the temperature of each cup.

4 Place the cups in sunlight. Predict what will happen to the liquids. Record your predictions. Observe the liquids every 10 minutes until the materials have melted. Record your observations.

My science notebook

WRAP IT UP!

1. **Predict** Did your results support your predictions? Explain.

2. **Analyze** How did the properties of the liquids change as they were cooled and heated?

EVAPORATION

Suppose you are outside on a rainy day. The air feels damp. Even though it is invisible, water vapor is in the air. Water can become water vapor through a change of state called **evaporation.**

The liquid water at the surface of the puddle is evaporating and becoming water vapor as it is heated.

voCAB

evaporation
(e-vap-uh-RĀ-shun)

Evaporation is the change from a liquid to a gas.

SUPPORTING STANDARD TEKS 3.5.C:
Predict, observe, and record changes in the
state of matter caused by heating or cooling.

Evaporation is a process in which matter changes from a liquid to a gas. Water can evaporate when it is heated. Evaporation can take place at many temperatures, but heat is always needed to cause evaporation.

Science in a Snap!

Evaporation

Use a dropper to put 5 drops of water on 2 paper squares. Predict which square will dry faster, a square in sunlight or a square in shade. Record your predictions.

Place one square in sunlight and the other in shade. Record how long it takes each square to dry.

? Did your results support your prediction? Why do you think water evaporated on one square faster than the other?

My science notebook

WRAP IT UP !

1. **Define** What is evaporation?

2. **Explain** Describe how matter changes state when a liquid, such as water, is heated.

3. **Apply** After a morning rain, you walk outside and see puddles on the ground. Later in the day, the puddles are gone. Explain how the water changed.

CONDENSATION

Look at the photo of the spider web. It did not rain, yet the spider web is wet. How could this happen? The spider web is covered with dew. Dew is water that forms during a process called **condensation.**

On a hot day, you may see water on the outside of a glass with a cold drink. These drops of water condensed from water vapor in the air.

voCAB

condensation
(kon-den-SĀ-shun)

Condensation is the change from a gas to a liquid.

SUPPORTING STANDARD TEKS 3.5.C:
Predict, observe, and record changes in the
state of matter caused by heating or cooling.

READY
SET
STAAR

Condensation is the change from a gas to a liquid. Condensation can happen when a gas is cooled. The cooler air around the spider web causes the water vapor in the air to condense and attach to the web.

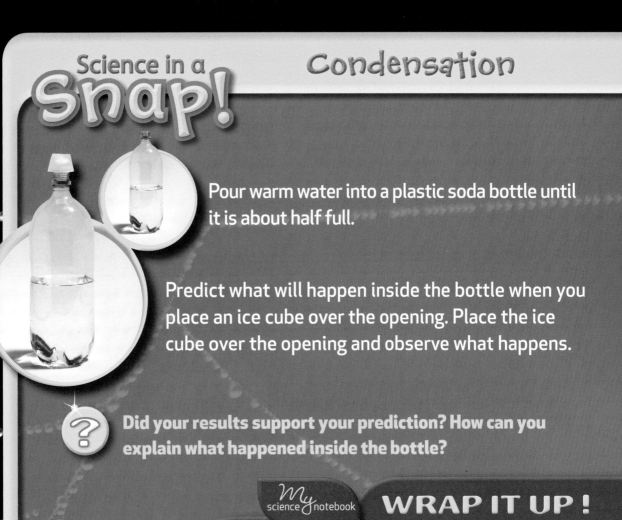

Science in a Snap!

Condensation

Pour warm water into a plastic soda bottle until it is about half full.

Predict what will happen inside the bottle when you place an ice cube over the opening. Place the ice cube over the opening and observe what happens.

? Did your results support your prediction? How can you explain what happened inside the bottle?

My science notebook

WRAP IT UP!

1. **Define** What is condensation?

2. **Explain** Describe what happens when a gas, such as water vapor, is cooled.

3. **Apply** You walk outside early in the morning and you see drops of water on the flowers. You know that it did not rain. How might the flowers have gotten wet?

11

CONSTRUCTION WORKER

Construction Workers

Buildings need to be made of solid materials. A hotel in northern Sweden is made out of ice! The hotel is built by construction workers.

The construction workers use packed snow to make the walls and ceilings of the ice hotel. Construction workers also cut large blocks of ice from a frozen river. These blocks are used to make pillars, beds, and other furniture.

When spring comes, the ice hotel melts. The water runs into the river. The next winter, the water in the river will freeze again. Construction workers will use it to build a new ice hotel.

TEKS 4.3.D:
Connect grade-level appropriate science
concepts with the history of science, science
careers, and contributions of scientists.

The columns and furniture are carved by construction workers from frozen blocks of ice taken from the nearby river.

Construction workers haul away large blocks of ice. They move ice from the river to the place where they will build the hotel.

This winch is an important machine on a sailboat. Part of a rope is wound around the winch. The other part of the rope is attached to the sail. When the crank on top of the winch is turned, force moves the rope and the sail into position. When the force of the wind pushes against the sail, the boat moves across the sea.

FORCE, MOTION, AND ENERGY

REPORTING CATEGORY 2: FORCE, MOTION, AND ENERGY

The student will demonstrate an understanding of force, motion, and energy and their relationships.

3.6 FORCE, MOTION, and ENERGY
The student knows that forces cause change and that energy exists in many forms.

SWINGS AND WAGONS

Look at the girl on the swing. She looks like she is having fun, but **work** is being done. Work is done when a force is used to move an object over a distance. The girl pushing her friend on the swing applies force to the swing. As the girl pushes the swing, the swing moves, and work is done.

The girl does work while pushing her friend on the swing. Force is applied to the swing to make it change position, or move.

vocAB

work
(WERK)

Work is done when a force is used to move an object over a distance.

SUPPORTING STANDARD TEKS 3.6.B: Demonstrate and observe how position and motion can be changed by pushing and pulling objects to show work being done such as swings, balls, pulleys, and wagons.

Work can be done with wagons, too. This woman is using a wagon to move heavy pots of flowers. The woman is using force to change the position of the wagon as she pulls it. Since the wagon moves as she pulls it, the woman is doing work. Any time that a force is used to move an object, work is being done.

The woman is doing work as she pulls the wagon. She is using a pulling force to change the position of the wagon.

WRAP IT UP!

My science notebook

1. **Define** What is work?

2. **Recall** Explain why pushing someone on a swing is an example of work being done.

3. **Apply** Construction workers are pushing a wheelbarrow with large rocks inside. Explain how moving the wheelbarrow is an example of work being done.

INVESTIGATE
MOTION OF A
MARBLE

 How does the amount of work a marble does change as its release height on a ramp changes?

Gravity, a force, is a pull. When gravity acts on an object, the object can change position, or move. When a force moves an object, work is being done. In this investigation, you can observe how different release heights on a ramp affect the amount of work a marble does.

MATERIALS

3 books   **foam tube**   **tape**   **plastic cup**   **marble**   **meterstick**

SUPPORTING STANDARD TEKS 3.6.B:
Demonstrate and observe how position and motion can be changed by pushing and pulling objects to show work being done such as swings, balls, pulleys, and wagons.

1

Place 3 books on the floor. Tape one end of a foam tube to the books. Tape the lower end of the tube to the floor. Place a plastic cup at the lower end of the tube.

2

My science notebook

Release a marble from the top of the tube. Observe the marble as it pushes the cup. Record your observations in your science notebook.

4

Tape the end of the tube to a chair. Predict how this change will affect how far the cup will move. Release the marble and measure how far the cup moves. Repeat twice.

3

Use a meterstick to measure how far the marble moves the cup. Record your observations. Repeat step 2 and measure the distance two more times.

My science notebook

WRAP IT UP!

1. **Predict** Did your results support your prediction? Explain.

2. **Compare** How did the height of the tube affect how much work was done by the marble?

19

PULLEYS

This laundry is drying in the Sun over a street in Italy. The laundry is drying on a rope that is connected to two **pulleys.** A pulley is a grooved wheel with a cable or rope running through the groove. When people pull on the rope, the position of the laundry changes. When the rope and the laundry are moved, the people are doing work.

pulley

voCAB

pulley
(PUL-lē)

A **pulley** is a grooved wheel with a cable or a rope running through the groove.

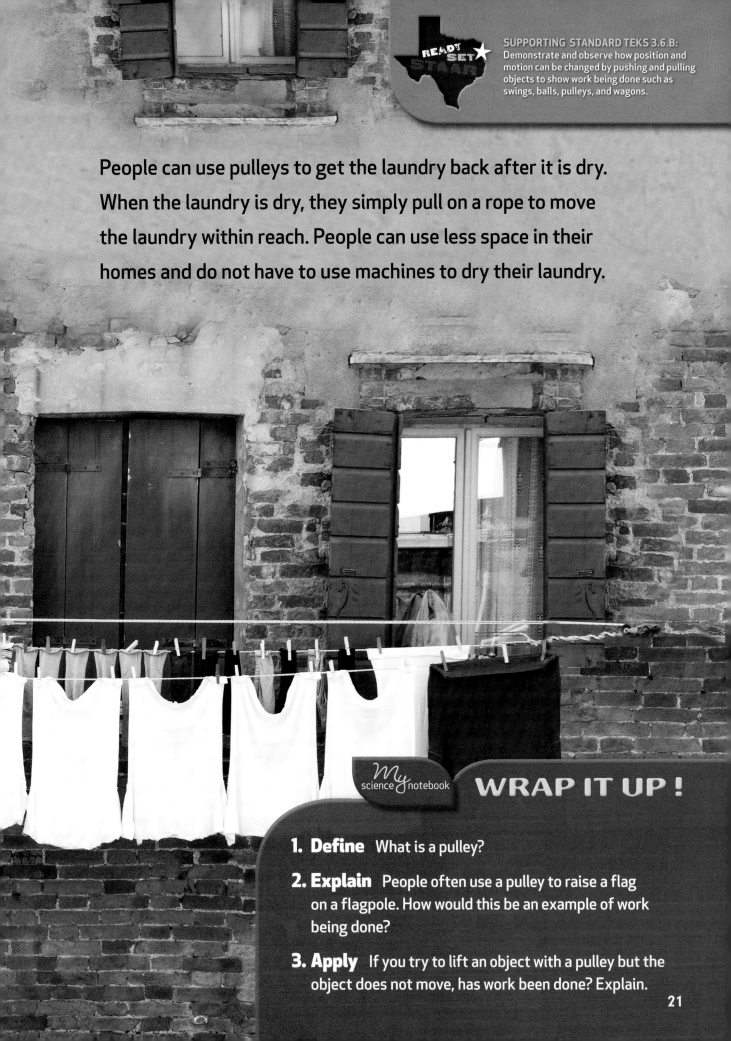

SUPPORTING STANDARD TEKS 3.6.B: Demonstrate and observe how position and motion can be changed by pushing and pulling objects to show work being done such as swings, balls, pulleys, and wagons.

People can use pulleys to get the laundry back after it is dry. When the laundry is dry, they simply pull on a rope to move the laundry within reach. People can use less space in their homes and do not have to use machines to dry their laundry.

My science notebook

WRAP IT UP!

1. **Define** What is a pulley?

2. **Explain** People often use a pulley to raise a flag on a flagpole. How would this be an example of work being done?

3. **Apply** If you try to lift an object with a pulley but the object does not move, has work been done? Explain.

PROFESSIONAL MOVER

Alston Glenn, Mover

Moving from your home to a new place can be a lot of work. You may have to move some heavy furniture. The workers who move furniture have to use a lot of different forces in a safe way. These experts are called movers!

Look at the photos of the movers doing work. The movers use a ramp to move heavy items into a truck. It is easier to move the box on a ramp than lifting it without a ramp.

The mover inside the truck uses a hand truck. It allows the mover to pull or push the heavy box on wheels instead of along the floor. The hand truck makes the job of moving heavy boxes easier.

When the movers move the boxes along the ramp with a force, they are doing work.

The hand truck allows movers to roll heavy boxes to where they need to go.

Mount Nyiragongo, in the Democratic Republic of the Congo, is one of the most active volcanoes on Earth. The crater usually contains a huge lake of hot, glowing lava. Since 1882, Mount Nyiragongo has erupted at least 34 times.

REPORTING CATEGORY 3

EARTH AND SPACE

REPORTING CATEGORY 3: EARTH AND SPACE

The student will demonstrate an understanding of components, cycles, patterns, and natural events of Earth and space systems.

4.7 EARTH and SPACE
The student knows that Earth consists of useful resources and its surface is constantly changing.

4.8 EARTH and SPACE
The student knows that there are recognizable patterns in the natural world and among the Sun, Earth, and Moon system.

RENEWABLE RESOURCES

You use **natural resources** every day. Natural resources are living and non-living things found on Earth that people need. For example, plants are natural resources. Some plants, such as corn, are grown for food. Other plants, such as cotton, are used to make material for clothing.

AIR
People can help keep air clean by driving less.

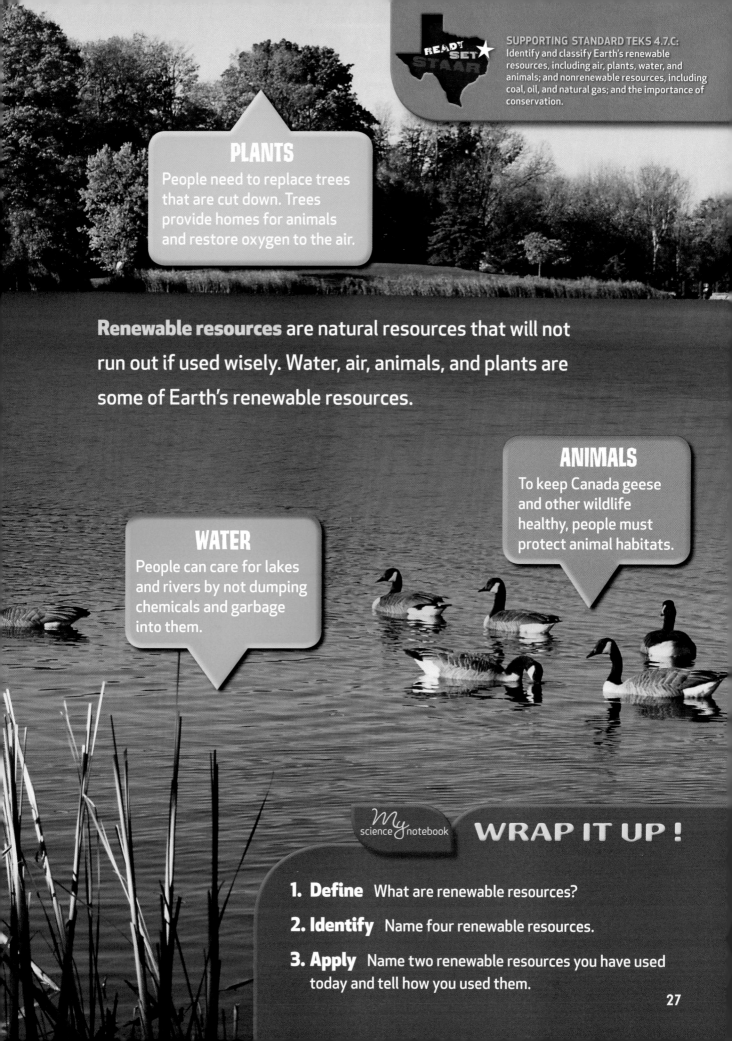

SUPPORTING STANDARD TEKS 4.7.C: Identify and classify Earth's renewable resources, including air, plants, water, and animals; and nonrenewable resources, including coal, oil, and natural gas; and the importance of conservation.

PLANTS

People need to replace trees that are cut down. Trees provide homes for animals and restore oxygen to the air.

Renewable resources are natural resources that will not run out if used wisely. Water, air, animals, and plants are some of Earth's renewable resources.

ANIMALS

To keep Canada geese and other wildlife healthy, people must protect animal habitats.

WATER

People can care for lakes and rivers by not dumping chemicals and garbage into them.

My science notebook

WRAP IT UP !

1. **Define** What are renewable resources?

2. **Identify** Name four renewable resources.

3. **Apply** Name two renewable resources you have used today and tell how you used them.

27

NONRENEWABLE RESOURCES

Nonrenewable resources are those resources that cannot be replaced quickly enough to keep them from running out. For example, **fossil fuels** are nonrenewable resources. Coal, oil, and natural gas are fossil fuels. Fossil fuels formed from plants and animals that lived millions of years ago. Earth's supply of fossil fuels can get used up.

voCAB

nonrenewable resources
(non-rē-NŪ-uh-bul RĒ-sors-es)

Nonrenewable resources cannot be replaced quickly enough to keep from running out.

fossil fuel
(FOS-ul FYŪ-ul)

A fossil fuel is a source of energy formed from plants and animals that lived millions of years ago.

Oil wells draw oil from the ground.

SUPPORTING STANDARD TEKS 4.7.C:
Identify and classify Earth's renewable
resources, including air, plants, water, and
animals; and nonrenewable resources, including
coal, oil, and natural gas; and the importance of
conservation.

Coal is used in power plants to produce electricity. Texas uses more coal for electricity than any other state. Fuel made from oil, such as gasoline and diesel, is used in cars and trucks. Natural gas is used to heat water and warm homes. Read the graph to learn more about how people in the United States use fossil fuels.

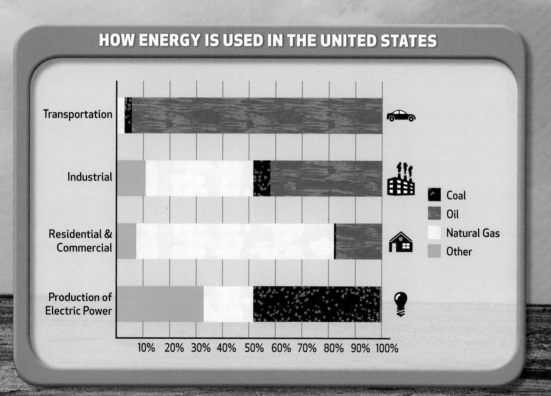

HOW ENERGY IS USED IN THE UNITED STATES

WRAP IT UP!

My science notebook

1. **Interpret Graphs** In the United States, which fossil fuels do people use for most of their electricity?

2. **Classify** Group the following natural resources as renewable or nonrenewable: coal, animals, water, plants, oil, natural gas, and air.

CONSERVING RESOURCES

People cannot survive without natural resources such as air, water, and plants. The careful use and protection of natural resources is known as **conservation.** Conservation is important. If nonrenewable resources such as fossil fuels get used up, they will be gone. Even renewable resources need to be used carefully. For example, people may cut down forests in order to produce lumber and other wood products. People need to plant new trees to replace the ones that they cut down.

HOW CAN YOU CONSERVE?

TURN OFF THE WATER.

COMPOST.

USE ALTERNATIVE TRANSPORTATION.

RECYCLE.

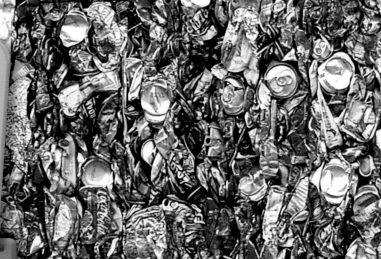

voCAB

conservation
(kon-suhr-VĀ-shun)

Conservation is the protection and care of natural resources.

Science in a Snap!

Recycle by the Numbers

Recycling is one way to conserve natural resources. Numbers on plastic products show the kind of plastic the object is made from. Most plastics that can be recycled have a 1 or 2.

Look for numbers on plastic objects. List them as 1, 2, or other numbers.

1	2
Food and Drink bottles	Bottles for non-food items
Food jars	Grocery Bags
Plastic Wrap	Playground equipment

What number was on most of the objects?
What other numbers did you find?

My science notebook   WRAP IT UP!

1. **Recall** What is conservation?

2. **Apply** Give three examples of things you can do to conserve natural resources.

3. **Evaluate** Trees are a renewable resource. Why is conserving forests important? Explain your answer.

SOIL PROPERTIES

Soil is important to people all over the world for growing plants for food. If you have ever planted a garden, you were digging in soil. Soil forms as rocks break down into smaller and smaller pieces. The pieces may be different sizes, such as the particles in sand or clay.

Soil contains pieces of rock as well as air and water. Soil may also contain humus, or bits of decayed plants and animals. Humus contains nutrients important for growing plants. Loam soil often contains humus.

SANDY SOIL

- Usually brown
- Feels rough and coarse; has larger grains than other soils
- Drains quickly; does not hold water well
- Some plants grow well in it

sandy soil

voCAB

soil
(SOIL)

Soil is a layer of loose materials on Earth's surface that is made up of rock particles, humus, air, and water.

humus
(HYŪ-mus)

Humus is a part of soil made of decayed plants and animals.

SUPPORTING STANDARD TEKS 4.7.A:
Examine properties of soils, including color and texture, capacity to retain water, and ability to support the growth of plants.

CLAY SOIL

clay soil

- Usually reddish
- Smooth; feels sticky when wet; has very small grains
- Drains slowly; holds water well
- Some plants grow well in it

LOAM SOIL

- Usually dark brown
- Feels smoother than sand but rougher than clay; has different grain sizes
- Drains well; holds some water
- Many plants grow well in it

loam soil

My science notebook — WRAP IT UP !

1. **Identify** Name some properties of soil.

2. **Evaluate** What property of soil do you think is most important to people? Explain your answer.

3. **Infer** Many plants grow well in loam soil. What soil properties do you think are important for supporting the growth of many kinds of plants?

33

INVESTIGATE

SOIL and WATER

 Which kind of soil holds the most water?

Trees, grasses, and most other plants need soil to grow. Farmers need soil to grow potatoes, corn, and other crops. But not all soil is the same. How much water soil can hold, or retain, is an important property of soil. It helps determine which plants can grow in that soil. In this investigation, you can examine how much water different kinds of soil retain.

MATERIALS

sandy soil   clay soil   loam   hand lens   3 cups with holes

3 cups without holes   pan balance   gram masses   graduated cylinder   water

SUPPORTING STANDARD TEKS 4.7.A:
Examine properties of soils, including color
and texture, capacity to retain water, and
ability to support the growth of plants.

1

Observe the properties of 3 kinds of soil with a hand lens, including color and texture. Record your observations in your science notebook. Then use a measuring cup to measure and pour 75 mL of each kind of soil into its own plastic cup with holes.

My science notebook

2

Use a pan balance and gram masses to find the mass of each cup of soil. Record your data.

3

Place each cup of soil inside a cup without holes. Then use a graduated cylinder to slowly pour 50 mL of water into each cup of soil.

4

Wait 10 minutes. Then use the balance to measure the mass of each cup of wet soil. Record your data. Subtract the mass of the cup with dry soil from the mass of the cup with wet soil to find out how much water each soil held.

My science notebook

WRAP IT UP !

1. **Compare** Share your results with other groups. Which soil type holds the most water?

2. **Infer** Why might soils that hold a medium amount of water be good for growing plants? Explain your answer.

EARTH'S SURFACE CAN CHANGE QUICKLY

Earth is covered with landforms that change over time. Some changes happen suddenly—within days or in just seconds. These are rapid changes. Some rapid changes are caused by activity deep inside Earth.

Earth has three main layers—the crust, the mantle, and the core. Read the diagram to learn about Earth's main layers.

EARTH'S LAYERS

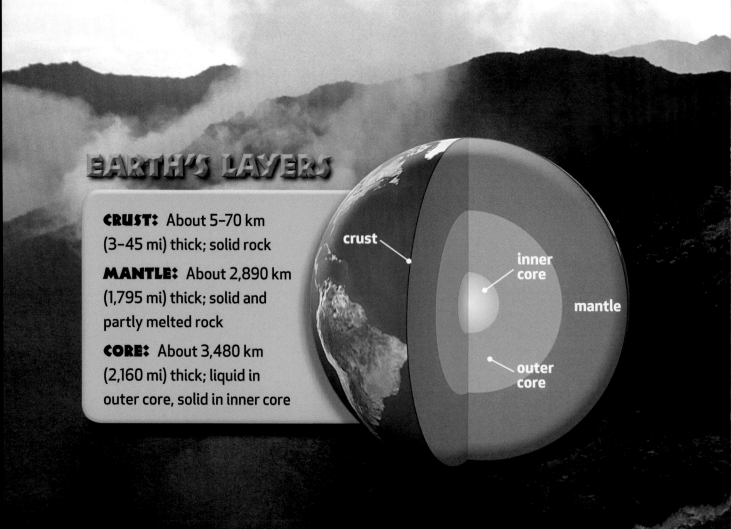

CRUST: About 5–70 km (3–45 mi) thick; solid rock

MANTLE: About 2,890 km (1,795 mi) thick; solid and partly melted rock

CORE: About 3,480 km (2,160 mi) thick; liquid in outer core, solid in inner core

crust

inner core

mantle

outer core

SUPPORTING STANDARD TEKS 3.7.B: Investigate rapid changes in Earth's surface such as volcanic eruptions, earthquakes, and landslides.

Changes in the crust and the mantle cause some of the rapid changes that occur in Earth's surface. The crust is the hard rocky part that you live on. Beneath the crust lies the mantle. The top part of the mantle is solid rock, like the crust. The rest of the mantle is partly melted rock. Next comes the core. The outer core is liquid. The inner core is solid.

Mauna Loa, on the island of Hawai'i, is Earth's largest volcano. Volcanoes cause rapid changes to Earth's surface.

My science notebook **WRAP IT UP!**

1. **List** What are Earth's three main layers?

2. **Explain** What can cause rapid changes in Earth's surface?

3. **Infer** How is a hard-boiled egg like the layers of Earth?

VOLCANOES

Magma is melted rock below Earth's surface. A volcano is an opening in Earth's crust through which magma erupts. Volcanic eruptions can cause rapid changes to the surface of Earth. When the hot magma spills onto Earth's surface, it is called lava. The lava cools and hardens into new, solid rock. The rock can build up and form a mountain. Hot ash and lava can cover the land, destroying buildings and burying towns. Volcanic ash can clog lakes and rivers and destroy crops.

In some places, visitors can get close to the lava that has just erupted from the Kilauea volcano. What will soon happen to the lava as it flows on Earth's surface?

SUPPORTING STANDARD TEKS 3.7.B:
Investigate rapid changes in Earth's surface
such as volcanic eruptions, earthquakes,
and landslides.

Volcanic eruptions can have some surprising effects on Earth's surface too. For example, ash from a volcano can become good soil for growing crops. Volcanoes can also create new landforms. The Hawaiian Islands formed as volcanoes built up from the floor of the Pacific Ocean.

Kilauea is the most active volcano in Hawai'i. The current eruption of Kilauea began on January 3, 1983.

My science notebook

WRAP IT UP!

1. **Explain** How do volcanic eruptions cause rapid changes on Earth's surface?

2. **Infer** How can volcanic eruptions form new land?

EARTHQUAKES

An earthquake is a rapid change in Earth's surface. Earthquakes are caused by the movement of Earth's **plates.** You can see Earth's plates in the map. Plates are huge sections of Earth's crust and upper mantle that move slowly on a layer of very hot rock. This movement causes faults to form. A fault is a break in Earth's surface where huge slabs of rock can move. Slabs of rock at the edges of faults often become locked together.

EARTH'S PLATES

The map shows Earth's major plates. The movement of plates can cause rapid changes in Earth's surface.

JUAN DE-FUCA PLATE

NORTH AMERICAN PLATE

EURASIAN PLATE

ARABIAN PLATE

PACIFIC PLATE

CARIBBEAN PLATE

PHILIPPINE PLATE

COCOS PLATE

AFRICAN PLATE

CAROLINE PLATE

PACIFIC PLATE

NAZCA PLATE

SOUTH AMERICAN PLATE

INDO-AUSTRALIAN PLATE

SCOTIA PLATE

ANTARCTIC PLATE

VOCAB

plate
(PLĀT)

A **plate** is a huge section of Earth's crust and upper mantle that moves slowly on a layer of very hot rock.

SUPPORTING STANDARD TEKS 3.7.B:
Investigate rapid changes in Earth's surface such as volcanic eruptions, earthquakes, and landslides.

When the slabs of rock break free, energy rapidly moves in all directions, making the ground shake. The violent shaking of some earthquakes can raise and lower the land or change the course of rivers. Strong earthquakes can damage buildings and other structures on Earth's surface too. Roads buckle, bridges collapse, and railroads twist.

The same 1992 earthquake damaged this home in Landers, California.

When a powerful earthquake happened in Southern California in 1992, Earth's crust separated along the fault.

My science *notebook*

WRAP IT UP!

1. **Cause and Effect** What causes many earthquakes?

2. **Explain** How can earthquakes cause rapid changes to Earth's surface?

3. **Interpret Maps** Do plate boundaries exist in the continents, the ocean floor, or both?

fault

INVESTIGATE

EARTHQUAKES

 How can you model one way earthquakes can happen?

At some faults, huge slabs of rock move as they push against each other. The huge slabs of rock can become locked together. Pressure builds. During an earthquake, the slabs of rock break free. The release of pressure moves the ground, causing rapid changes in Earth's surface. In this investigation, you can use a model to learn about events such as earthquakes that you can't study up close.

MATERIALS

2 spiral notebooks

SUPPORTING STANDARD TEKS 3.7.B:
Investigate rapid changes in Earth's surface
such as volcanic eruptions, earthquakes,
and landslides.

1

Place 2 spiral notebooks side-by-side so the spirals are touching. Predict what will happen when the notebooks scrape past each other. Record your prediction in your science notebook.

My science *notebook*

2

Place a hand on top of each notebook. Slowly push them in opposite directions. Record your observations.

3

Place the 2 spiral notebooks side-by-side again. Predict what will happen if you push the notebooks together while moving them in opposite directions. Record your prediction.

4

Place a hand firmly on top of each notebook. Slowly push them in opposite directions, using more force. Record your observations.

My science *notebook*

WRAP IT UP !

1. **Predict** Did your results support your predictions? Explain.

2. **Explain** Describe how rapid changes to Earth's surface can happen when pressure builds between huge slabs of rock along faults.

43

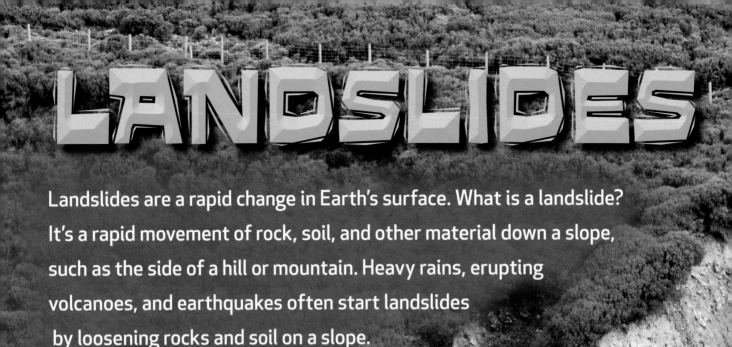

LANDSLIDES

Landslides are a rapid change in Earth's surface. What is a landslide? It's a rapid movement of rock, soil, and other material down a slope, such as the side of a hill or mountain. Heavy rains, erupting volcanoes, and earthquakes often start landslides by loosening rocks and soil on a slope. The force of gravity then pulls the material downhill.

Landslides are common on steep river banks.

SUPPORTING STANDARD TEKS 3.7.B:
Investigate rapid changes in Earth's surface
such as volcanic eruptions, earthquakes,
and landslides.

Landslides sometimes move large amounts of rocks and soil. The shape of hills and mountains on Earth's surface may change in just a few minutes. The rocks and soil collect at the bottom of the slope.

 Like earthquakes, landslides can be damaging. This highway in Taiwan was crushed under tons of rock and soil. The landslide happened rapidly and without warning.

My science notebook **WRAP IT UP!**

1. **Identify** What happens during a landslide?

2. **Explain** How is a landslide a rapid change in Earth's surface?

3. **Infer** How might a volcano trigger a landslide?

45

WEATHER AND WEATHER MAPS

Weather maps are used to help explain what the **weather** is like and predict what it will be like in the future. Weather is the state of the atmosphere at a certain place and time. Weather events, such as the thunderstorm shown in the picture, happen at a front. A front is a boundary where two different large air masses meet.

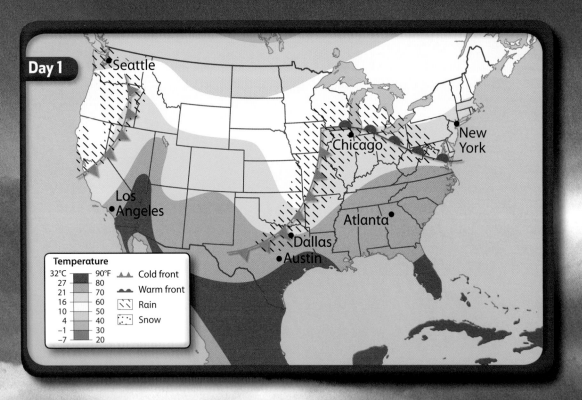

Day 1

Seattle
Chicago
New York
Los Angeles
Atlanta
Dallas
Austin

Temperature

32°C	90°F
27	80
21	70
16	60
10	50
4	40
−1	30
−7	20

Cold front
Warm front
Rain
Snow

You can learn about the weather by looking at a weather map.

SUPPORTING STANDARD TEKS 4.8.A:
Measure and record changes in weather and
make predictions using weather maps, weather
symbols, and a map key.

READY
SET
STAAR

In the United States, most weather patterns move from west to
east. Look at the two weather maps on these pages. Weather
maps use symbols to report data about the weather. The maps
include a key that shows you what the weather symbols mean.
How did weather conditions change from Day 1 to Day 2?

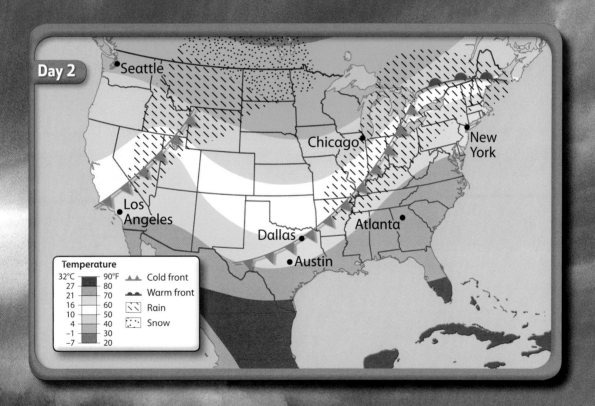

Day 2

Seattle

Chicago

New
York

Los
Angeles

Dallas

Atlanta

Austin

Temperature

32°C	90°F
27	80
21	70
16	60
10	50
4	40
−1	30
−7	20

▲▲ Cold front

⌒⌒ Warm front

Rain

Snow

My
science notebook

WRAP IT UP!

1. **Interpret Maps** What do the blue curving lines on the
   map stand for?

2. **Predict** Find a place on the weather maps. Use the
   maps and map key to predict what the weather will be
   like there on the third day. Explain your answer.

47

INVESTIGATE
WEATHER

 How can you measure changes in wind speed and temperature?

Scientists use weather instruments to measure changes in weather. In this investigation, you can use an anemometer to measure wind speed and a thermometer to measure temperature.

MATERIALS

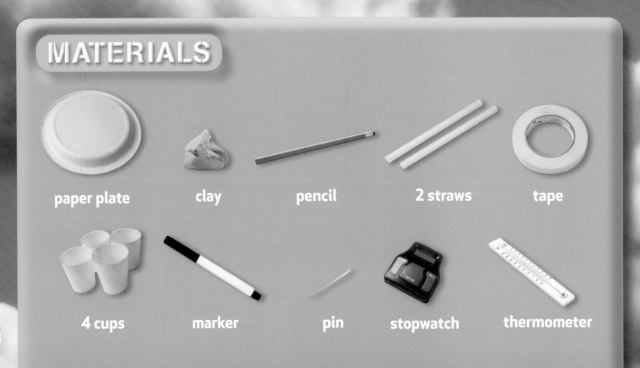

| paper plate | clay | pencil | 2 straws | tape |
| 4 cups | marker | pin | stopwatch | thermometer |

SUPPORTING STANDARD TEKS 4.8.A: Measure and record changes in weather and make predictions using weather maps, weather symbols, and a map key.

1 Follow your teacher's instructions for making an anemometer.

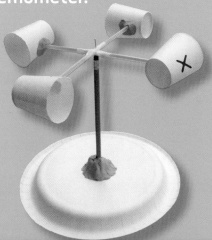

2 *My science notebook*

Place the anemometer in a clear space outside. To estimate how fast the wind is blowing, count the number of times the cup with the **X** spins around in 1 minute. Use a stopwatch. Record the data in your science notebook.

3 Use a thermometer to measure the air temperature. Record the temperature in degrees Celsius.

4 Repeat steps 2 and 3 at the same time each day for 1 week. Look for changes in the wind speed and temperature.

My science notebook **WRAP IT UP!**

1. **Summarize** How did the data for wind speed and temperature change during the week?

2. **Explain** How did your weather tools help you to measure the weather conditions?

EVAPORATION
IN THE WATER CYCLE

Water is a renewable natural resource because Earth renews its water in the water cycle. The water cycle is the continuous movement of water from Earth's surface to the air and back again. All living things use water to stay alive. Yet because of the water cycle, Earth's supply of water never runs out.

voCAB

water cycle
(WAH-tur SĪ-kul)

The water cycle is the movement of water from Earth's surface to the air and back again.

evaporation
(i-vap-uh-RĀ-shun)

Evaporation is the change from a liquid to a gas.

SUPPORTING STANDARD TEKS 4.8.B:
Describe and illustrate the continuous
movement of water above and on the surface of
Earth through the water cycle and explain the
role of the Sun as a major source of energy in
this process.

Energy from the Sun powers the water cycle. The Sun's energy causes some of Earth's water to heat up and **evaporate.** When water evaporates, it forms a gas called water vapor. In the water cycle, water moves from Earth's surface to the air by evaporation.

Sun

Evaporation

As the water on Earth's surface heats up, some of it evaporates. The Sun's energy provides the heat that is needed for evaporation to occur.

My science notebook **WRAP IT UP!**

1. **Explain** What happens to water when it evaporates?

2. **Describe** Describe the Sun's role in the water cycle.

3. **Infer** Why is the water cycle important for living things on Earth?

CONDENSATION
IN THE WATER CYCLE

As water vapor in the air rises, it cools. The cooler temperatures lead to **condensation**. Condensation is the changing of a gas into a liquid. In the water cycle, condensation is the change of water vapor from a gas into tiny drops of water. If the air is cold enough, the water vapor turns into tiny crystals of ice.

WHAT'S IN A RAINDROP?

About 1 million tiny water droplets are needed to make just one raindrop.

VOCAB

condensation
(kon-den-SĀ-shun)

Condensation is the change from a gas to a liquid.

SUPPORTING STANDARD TEKS 4.8.B:
Describe and illustrate the continuous
movement of water above and on the surface
of Earth through the water cycle and explain
the role of the Sun as a major source of energy
in this process.

The ice crystals or water droplets are so small that they float on air. When enough of them collect, they form clouds. A cloud has millions of ice crystals and water droplets. Formation of clouds is necessary for water to continue moving through the water cycle.

When water condenses, it changes from water vapor to liquid water.

My science notebook   WRAP IT UP!

1. **Describe**   Describe how clouds usually form.

2. **Contrast**   How are condensation and evaporation different from each other?

3. **Infer**   Suppose the temperature of water vapor does not change as the water vapor rises. Explain whether clouds will form.

PRECIPITATION
IN THE WATER CYCLE

Ice crystals or water droplets in clouds can swirl around and grow. When many water droplets or ice crystals come together in clouds, they can stick together and become heavy. Then they fall to Earth as **precipitation.** Observe different kinds of precipitation in the chart.

TYPES OF PRECIPITATION

Rain is liquid water.

Flakes of ice are snow.

Small pieces of ice are sleet.

Lumps of ice are hail.

Water droplets from the clouds are falling to Earth as precipitation.

voCAB

precipitation
(pri-sip-uh-TĀ-shun)

Precipitation is water that falls from a cloud.

SUPPORTING STANDARD TEKS 4.8.B:
Describe and illustrate the continuous
movement of water above and on the surface of
Earth through the water cycle and explain the
role of the Sun as a major source of energy in
this process.

Rain, snow, sleet, and hail are some types of precipitation
in the water cycle. The type of precipitation depends on
the temperature of clouds and the temperature of the air
between the clouds and the ground.

Precipitation is water that falls from clouds toward Earth's surface in the
water cycle.

WRAP IT UP !

1. **Describe** Describe what can happen in the water cycle
   after water vapor condenses to form clouds.

2. **Infer** Can precipitation occur without clouds? Explain.

RUNOFF IN THE WATER CYCLE

Most of the precipitation that falls from clouds just evaporates. Some precipitation that does not evaporate soaks through the surface of Earth and becomes groundwater. Groundwater is water that collects in cracks and soil below Earth's surface. Groundwater flows slowly. It eventually returns to rivers and lakes through underground pathways. It can then evaporate and make its trip through the water cycle again.

This is the Godafoss waterfall in Iceland. Waterfalls occur wherever rivers flow over cliffs.

voCAB

runoff
(RUN-awf)

Runoff is water that flows on the surface of Earth.

SUPPORTING STANDARD TEKS 4.8.B:
Describe and illustrate the continuous
movement of water above and on the surface
of Earth through the water cycle and explain
the role of the Sun as a major source of energy
in this process.

Other water becomes **runoff.** Runoff is water that does not sink into the soil. It flows freely over the surface of Earth. Runoff eventually collects into streams and other bodies of water, such as lakes, ponds, and the ocean.

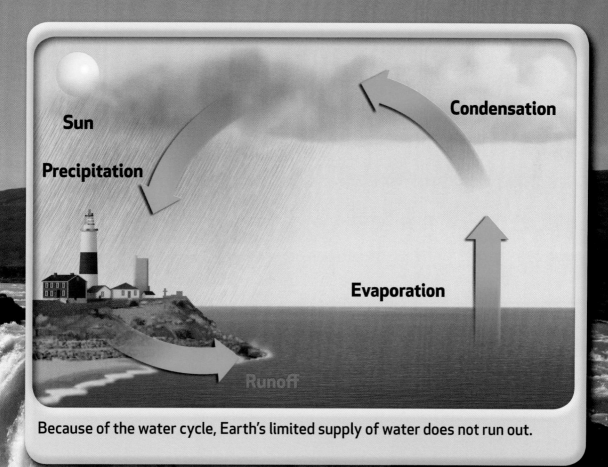

Because of the water cycle, Earth's limited supply of water does not run out.

WRAP IT UP!

My science notebook

1. **Describe** Describe what eventually happens to runoff.

2. **Contrast** Explain the difference between runoff and groundwater.

3. **Summarize** Draw a picture of the water cycle. Describe the movement of water above and on Earth's surface.

57

THE SOLAR SYSTEM

What is the solar system? The solar system includes the Sun and all of the objects that **revolve,** or travel in a path, around it. The Sun is our closest star. It is also the largest object in the solar system. Next in size are the eight planets. The diagram shows the order of the planets from the Sun. The distances between them are much greater than shown here.

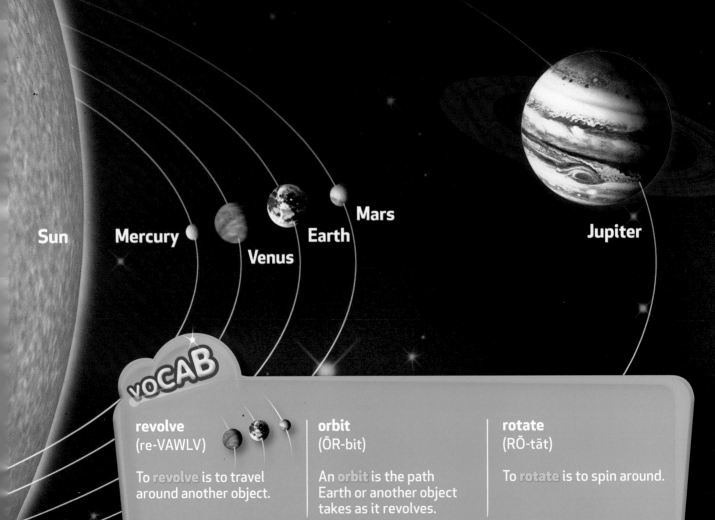

Sun   Mercury   Venus   Earth   Mars   Jupiter

voCAB

revolve
(re-VAWLV)

To **revolve** is to travel around another object.

orbit
(ŌR-bit)

An **orbit** is the path Earth or another object takes as it revolves.

rotate
(RŌ-tāt)

To **rotate** is to spin around.

The planets in order of their distances from the Sun are Mercury, Venus, Earth, Mars, Jupiter, Saturn, Uranus, and Neptune. Each planet revolves around the Sun in a path called its **orbit.** As the planets revolve around the Sun, they move in another way, too. They **rotate,** or spin around.

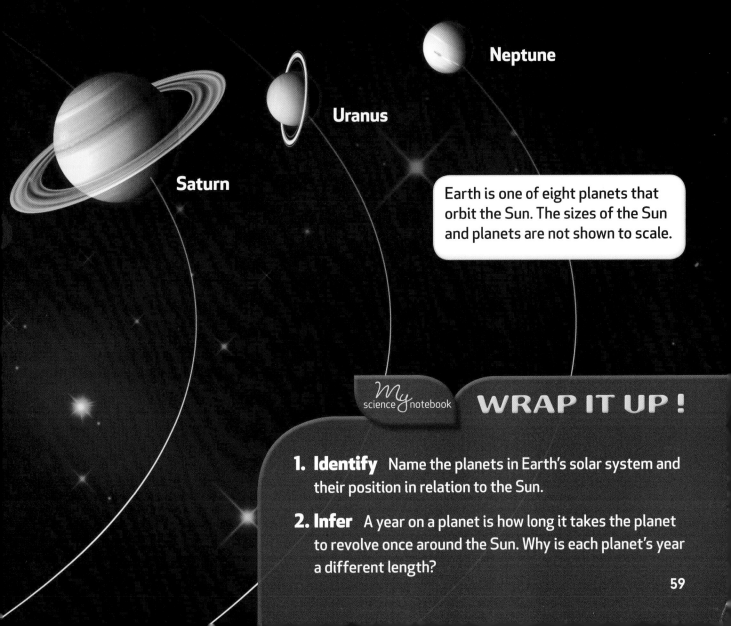

Neptune

Uranus

Saturn

Earth is one of eight planets that orbit the Sun. The sizes of the Sun and planets are not shown to scale.

My science notebook

WRAP IT UP!

1. **Identify**   Name the planets in Earth's solar system and their position in relation to the Sun.

2. **Infer**   A year on a planet is how long it takes the planet to revolve once around the Sun. Why is each planet's year a different length?

INVESTIGATE
SHADOWS

How does a shadow caused by sunlight change?

Earth's rotation causes patterns in the natural world that you can observe. As Earth spins, the Sun appears to move across the sky. Shadows on Earth's surface change in length and direction. The ways in which shadows change form a pattern. In this investigation, you can measure how shadows caused by sunlight change during the day.

MATERIALS

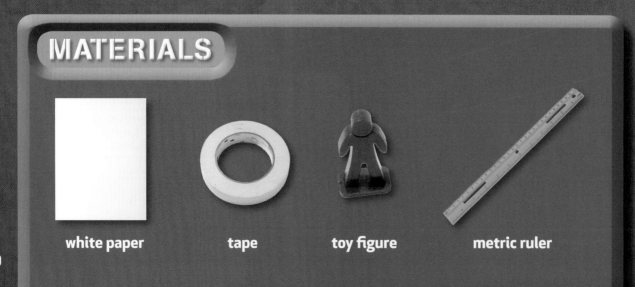

white paper   tape   toy figure   metric ruler

SUPPORTING STANDARD TEKS 4.8.C:
Collect and analyze data to identify sequences
and predict patterns of change in shadows,
tides, seasons, and the observable appearance
of the Moon over time.

1

Tape a sheet of paper in a
sunny spot. Put a toy figure
near the center edge of
the paper. Observe the
shadow the toy makes.

2

Put an *X* to show where you
would look to find the Sun. Trace
the toy's shadow on the paper.
Write the date and the time by
the X and by the shadow outline.

3

My
science notebook

Use a metric ruler to measure
the length of the shadow. Record
your measurement in your science
notebook.

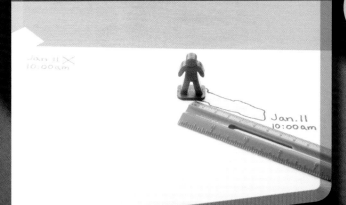

4

Repeat steps 2 and 3 three
more times during the day.
Observe how the shadows
change throughout the day.

My
science notebook

WRAP IT UP !

1. **Identify** What pattern in length and movement did you observe
   with the shadows?

2. **Predict** How will the shadows change if you repeat the
   investigation starting earlier in the day?

SEASONS

What season will it be at this time next year? If you said the same one, you're right. The seasons make a pattern. The four seasons—summer, fall, winter, and spring—repeat in the same sequence year after year.

The table on the next page has data about patterns of change through the seasons in Fort Worth, Texas.

fall

winter

spring

In Texas, length of daylight is shorter in fall than in summer.

It's a chilly day in Fort Worth! Winter days have the fewest hours of daylight.

In spring, length of daylight increases every day.

SUPPORTING STANDARD TEKS 4.8.C:
Collect and analyze data to identify sequences and predict patterns of change in shadows, tides, seasons, and the observable appearance of the Moon over time.

SEASONAL PATTERNS IN FORT WORTH, TEXAS

	FALL (Sept. 22–Dec. 21)	WINTER (Dec. 22–Mar 19)	SPRING (Mar. 20–June 20)	SUMMER (June 21–Sept. 21)
AVERAGE HIGH TEMPERATURE	23°C (73°F)	15°C (59°F)	26°C (79°F)	35°C (95°F)
AVERAGE LOW TEMPERATURE	10°C (50°F)	2°C (36°F)	14°C (57°F)	21°C (70°F)
AVERAGE LENGTH OF DAYLIGHT	11 h	10 h 45 min	13 h 20 min	13 h 33 min
AVERAGE PRECIPITATION	5.88 cm (2.31 in)	4.02 cm (1.58 in)	7.08 cm (2.79 in)	4.77 cm (1.88 in)

Summer in Fort Worth, Texas

summer

It's a hot day in Fort Worth. Average temperature and length of daylight are greatest in summer.

My science notebook

WRAP IT UP!

1. **Sequence** In what order do the seasons occur?

2. **Predict** What will happen to the length of day as spring turns into summer?

3. **Research** Choose another location, such as your home town. Research how the length of daylight changes. Plot the data in a graph.

63

MOON PHASES

The pictures show eight **phases** of the Moon and the sequence in which they occur. A phase is how the Moon appears from Earth. It takes the Moon about four weeks to go through all of its phases. Some days the Moon looks like a full circle, other days like part of a circle. But the Moon doesn't really change shape. It's always shaped like a sphere, or ball.

NEW MOON

CRESCENT MOON

FIRST QUARTER MOON

GIBBOUS MOON

MOON MOVES

The Moon rotates once in about four weeks, the same amount of time it takes to revolve around Earth. For that reason, we always see the same side of the Moon.

VOCAB

phase
(FĀZ)

A **phase** is how the Moon appears from Earth.

READY SET STAAR

SUPPORTING STANDARD TEKS 4.8.C:
Collect and analyze data to identify sequences
and predict patterns of change in shadows,
tides, seasons, and the observable appearance
of the Moon over time.

What changes is how much of the Moon's lighted half you can see from Earth. Half of the Moon faces the Sun. The Sun lights that side of the Moon. How much of the lighted half you see depends on where the Moon is in its revolution around Earth.

FULL MOON   GIBBOUS MOON   THIRD QUARTER MOON   CRESCENT MOON

My science notebook

WRAP IT UP !

1. **Sequence**   Name eight phases of the Moon beginning with the New Moon.

2. **Predict**   Suppose today there is a Full Moon. What phase will the Moon be in about eight weeks from now?

65

INVESTIGATE MOON PHASES

 How does the lighted part of the Moon seem to change?

In this investigation, you can observe a model of how the lighted part of the Moon appears to change shape during the month.

NEW MOON	CRESCENT MOON	FIRST QUARTER MOON	GIBBOUS MOON

FULL MOON	GIBBOUS MOON	THIRD QUARTER MOON	CRESCENT MOON

MATERIALS

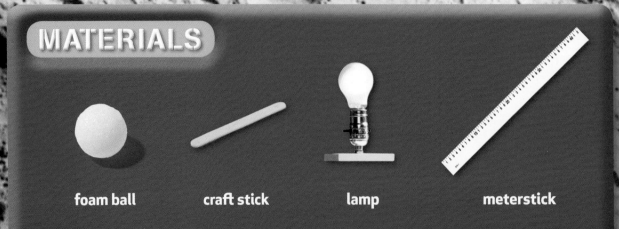

foam ball   craft stick   lamp   meterstick

SUPPORTING STANDARD TEKS 4.8.C:
Collect and analyze data to identify sequences and predict patterns of change in shadows, tides, seasons, and the observable appearance of the Moon over time.

1

Push a craft stick into a foam ball. The ball is a model of the Moon. Place a lamp at eye level. The lamp represents the Sun. Stand 2 meters from the lamp and hold the craft stick. Face the lamp. You represent Earth.

2

Turn one quarter of a turn to your left. Observe the ball. Draw your observations in your science notebook. Match your drawing to a Moon phase picture.

3

Repeat step 2. With each turn, draw your observations of the ball. Match each drawing to a Moon phase picture.

4

Complete your turn and face the lamp again. Draw your observations of the ball. Match your drawing to a Moon phase picture.

WRAP IT UP!

1. **Sequence** Draw eight phases of the moon in the order in which they happen.

2. **Predict** What pattern will you observe if you repeat this activity but begin by facing away from the lamp?

TIDES

Along coasts, water rises up over the shore and then slowly falls back again in a pattern. This daily rise and fall of ocean waters is known as tides. When the water rises to its highest level, it is at high tide. Then the water falls until it is at its lowest level, which is low tide. Most coastal places have two tide cycles each day.

At high tide, these rocks and all the organisms living on them will be covered with water.

SUPPORTING STANDARD TEKS 4.8.C:
Collect and analyze data to identify sequences
and predict patterns of change in shadows,
tides, seasons, and the observable appearance
of the Moon over time.

What causes tides? The Moon's gravity has an effect on Earth—
it pulls on Earth's water. This causes high tide on the side of Earth
that is closest to the Moon. High tide also happens on the side
farthest from the Moon. The Moon's gravity pulls Earth away
from the water on that side. Low tide happens everywhere else.
In most areas two high tides and two low tides happen each day.

My science notebook

WRAP IT UP!

1. **Sequence** Describe the pattern of tides over a period
   of one day.

2. **Predict** If a low tide occurs at noon, what kind of tide
   will happen at about midnight?

Twice a day at Saint Michael's Mount, the water level rises in a high tide. Twice a day, the water level lowers in a low tide. The tides happen in a sequence: high tide, low tide, high tide, low tide. The graph shows the pattern of high tide and low tide over a period of 24 hours. People can use a graph like this one to predict changes in tides.

High tide happens on the side of Earth that is closest to the Moon. The Moon's gravity pulls Earth's water. High tide also happens on the side farthest from the Moon. The Moon's gravity pulls Earth away from the water on that side. Low tide happens everywhere else.

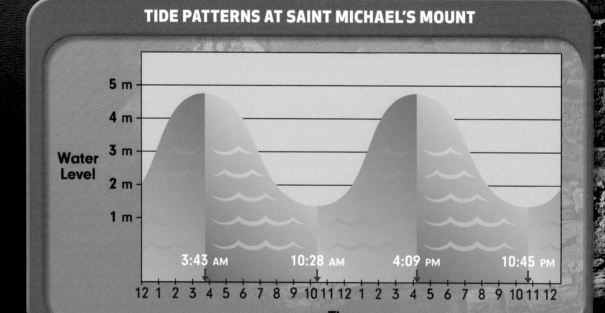

TIDE PATTERNS AT SAINT MICHAEL'S MOUNT

SUPPORTING STANDARD TEKS 4.8.C:
Collect and analyze data to identify
sequences and predict patterns of change in
shadows, tides, seasons, and the observable
appearance of the Moon over time.

READY
SET
STAAR

road →

low tide

← road

SHARE AND COMPARE

At high tide, Saint Michael's Mount in Cornwall, England, is an island.

- Study the tide graph. What times of the day did high tides happen? What times of the day did low tides happen?

- Do research to find out more about tides at Percé Rock, Canada, and Mont Saint-Michel, France. Share your information with a group that chose a different location.

METEOROLOGIST

Sepi Yalda

For Sepi Yalda, the sky is a puzzle. How does it change—and how can we predict those changes? Yalda teaches meteorology, the study of weather and the atmosphere. How did Yalda get interested in meteorology? She liked to solve puzzles about weather.

Every day, meteorologists answer one big question— what will the weather be like? To get the answer, they collect data and use computers to make predictions.

BALLOON BLAST!

Worldwide, almost 1,800 weather balloons are released every day. Weather balloons can rise quickly—about 300 meters (1,000 feet) per minute. At about 30 kilometers (100,000 feet), low air pressure can cause them to burst.

READY SET STAAR

TEKS 4.3.D:
Connect grade-level appropriate science concepts with the history of science, science careers, and contributions of scientists.

Meteorologists do more than predict the weather. They also experiment with ways to decrease air pollution. They provide data that help engineers design buildings and roads, and help farmers plan crops. Meteorologists also warn people about storms, floods, and hurricanes.

Meteorologists use weather balloons to measure wind speed, humidity, air pressure, and temperature far above Earth's surface.

The coyote can be found throughout North and Central America. Coyotes can live in forests, deserts, grasslands, and near big cities. Coyotes eat almost anything—small animals, fruits, vegetables, or even garbage. Coyotes make high-pitched howling noises that are most often heard at dusk or nighttime.

ORGANISMS AND ENVIRONMENTS

REPORTING CATEGORY 4: ORGANISMS AND ENVIRONMENTS

The student will demonstrate an understanding of the structures and functions of living organisms and their interdependence on each other and on their environment.

3.9 ORGANISMS and ENVIRONMENTS
The student knows that organisms have characteristics that help them survive and can describe patterns, cycles, systems, and relationships within the environments.

3.10 ORGANISMS and ENVIRONMENTS
The student knows that organisms undergo similar life processes and have structures that help them survive within their environments.

GRASSLAND ECOSYSTEMS

One type of environment found in Texas is a grassland. Grasslands are areas covered with mostly grasses and few trees. Organisms, or living things, in the grassland interact with each other and with the non-living things in an **ecosystem.** An ecosystem is all the living and non-living things in an area.

bison

voCAB

ecosystem
(Ē-kō-sis-tum)

An ecosystem is all the living and non-living things in an area.

SUPPORTING STANDARD TEKS 3.9.A: Observe and describe the physical characteristics of environments and how they support populations and communities within an ecosystem.

The organisms in this photograph interact with the non-living things in their environment. Animals breathe air and drink water. Plants grow in soil. Plants get energy directly from the Sun to make their own food. These organisms also interact with other living things in their environment. The bison and the prairie dog eat plants to get energy. Other animals eat animals to get energy they need to live and grow. Ecosystems, such as this grassland, provide for the needs of the organisms.

All organisms depend on their ecosystem for food, water, space, and air to survive.

prairie dog

My science notebook

WRAP IT UP !

1. **Define** What is an ecosystem?

2. **Apply** Describe the living and non-living things in this grassland ecosystem. Tell how organisms that live there are supported by their ecosystem.

77

GRASSLAND POPULATIONS and COMMUNITIES

Many Texas grassland ecosystems have prairie dogs. All of the prairie dogs living in the grassland ecosystem are called a population. A population is all the individuals of a species that live in an area. The population of prairie dogs gets what it needs, including water, food, space, and air, from its ecosystem.

INDIVIDUAL
A single organism, such as this prairie dog, is an individual in an ecosystem.

POPULATION
All the prairie dogs that live in the grassland are a population.

voCAB

population
(pop-yū-LĀ-shun)

A population is all the individuals of a species that live in an area.

community
(kuh-MYŪ-nuh-tē)

A community is made up of all the different populations that live and interact in an area.

SUPPORTING STANDARD TEKS 3.9.A:
Observe and describe the physical
characteristics of environments and
how they support populations and
communities within an ecosystem.

Many different populations live in a grassland. All the different populations that live and interact in an area make up a **community.** The populations of prairie dogs, bison, coyotes, and plants are parts of the grassland community shown here. The grassland populations and communities are supported by the physical characteristics of the environment. They find what they need to survive in their grassland ecosystem.

COMMUNITY
All the populations of organisms that live and interact in the grassland form a community.

ECOSYSTEM
All the organisms in this grassland get what they need to survive from their environment.

My science notebook   WRAP IT UP!

1. **Compare** How is a community different from a population?

2. **Infer** What are some of the physical characteristics you can observe or infer in these photos of a grassland?

3. **Explain** How do the physical characteristics of an environment help support the organisms that live there?

79

Life Cycle of a Jalapeño Pepper Plant

Many flowering plants go through similar stages of life. The series of stages that a jalapeño pepper plant goes through during its lifetime is its life cycle. Follow the diagram of the life cycle of the jalapeño pepper plant as you read. Then review the life stages of a tomato plant that are shown below.

Many jalapeño peppers are grown in the states of Texas and New Mexico.

Life Stages of a Tomato Plant

Seed   **Seedling**   **Young Plant**   **Adult Plant**

SUPPORTING STANDARD TEKS 3.10.C:
Investigate and compare how animals and
plants undergo a series of orderly changes
in their diverse life cycles such as tomato
plants, frogs, and ladybugs.

Adult Plant

Flowers can grow on an adult jalapeño pepper plant. The flowers may produce fruit called jalapeño peppers.

Seed

Each jalapeño pepper fruit holds many seeds.

Life Cycle of a Jalapeño Pepper Plant

Seedling

Given the proper soil temperature and moisture, a jalapeño pepper seed can grow into a seedling.

Young Plant

The seedling grows into a young jalapeño pepper plant.

My science notebook

WRAP IT UP!

1. **Define** What is a life cycle?

2. **Compare** How are the life stages of a jalapeño pepper plant and a tomato plant alike?

81

INVESTIGATE
The Life Cycle of a Bean Plant

> **?** How does a bean plant change during its life cycle?

Organisms go through many changes. The stages that an organism goes through during its lifetime are called a life cycle. In this investigation, you will observe the changes that occur during the life cycle of a bean plant.

MATERIALS

hand lens

3 bean seeds

cup with soil

spoon

SUPPORTING STANDARD TEKS 3.10.C:
Investigate and compare how animals and plants undergo a series of orderly changes in their diverse life cycles such as tomato plants, frogs, and ladybugs.

1

Observe bean plant seeds with a hand lens. Record your observations in your science notebook. Use a spoon to plant 3 bean seeds in a cup with soil.

2

When the seeds sprout into seedlings, observe and draw the plant parts. Continue to observe and draw plants over time. Record your observations.

3

When flowers form, use a hand lens to examine the parts of each flower. Draw the flowers.

4

Continue to observe the flowers until pods form. Open the pods to observe new bean seeds.

WRAP IT UP!

1. **Explain** What changes did you observe in the plant as it grew?

2. **Compare** How are the life cycles of the bean and jalapeño pepper plants alike? How are they different?

Life Cycle
of a
Rhinoceros Beetle

A rhinoceros beetle is a large insect with a horn-like structure on its head. During the life cycle of a rhinoceros beetle, it goes through four stages. At each of these stages, it looks very different. Follow the diagram of the life cycle of the rhinoceros beetle as you read. Then review the life stages of a ladybug that are shown below.

Life Stages of a Ladybug

| Egg | Larva | Pupa | Adult |

SUPPORTING STANDARD TEKS 3.10.C:
Investigate and compare how animals and
plants undergo a series of orderly changes
in their diverse life cycles such as tomato
plants, frogs, and ladybugs.

Life Cycle of a Rhinoceros Beetle

Egg
An adult female rhinoceros beetle lays eggs in warm soil.

Adult
The adult has different body parts from the pupa. These include wings and a horn.

Larva
The larva hatches from an egg. It grows into a large white grub.

Pupa
Just like a ladybug, the rhinoceros beetle changes form during the pupa stage. The pupa has a hard shell. The pupa changes into an adult.

WRAP IT UP!

1. **Contrast** Describe some differences between the pupa stage and the adult stage of the rhinoceros beetle.

2. **Compare** How are the life stages of the rhinoceros beetle similar to the life stages of a ladybug?

LIFE CYCLE OF A NEWT

The great crested newt is a long, black amphibian. The great crested newt can grow up to 18 cm (7 in.) in length and live as long as 15 years! Follow the diagram of the life cycle of the great crested newt as you read. Then review the life stages of a frog that are shown below.

The great crested newt can be found in northwestern Europe.

LIFE STAGES OF A FROG

Egg   Tadpole   Young Frog   Adult

SUPPORTING STANDARD TEKS 3.10.C: Investigate and compare how animals and plants undergo a series of orderly changes in their diverse life cycles such as tomato plants, frogs, and ladybugs.

LIFE CYCLE OF A NEWT

Egg

An adult female great crested newt lays an egg on a leaf and folds the leaf to protect the egg.

Adult

An adult great crested newt lives on land and breathes air.

Larva

A great crested newt larva has a tail and no legs. It lives in water and breathes through gills.

Young Newt

The young great crested newt grows legs. The newt continues to live under water.

WRAP IT UP !

My science *notebook*

1. **Contrast**   Describe some differences between the larva and the adult stages of the great crested newt.

2. **Compare**   How are the life stages of the great crested newt similar to the life stages of a frog?

87

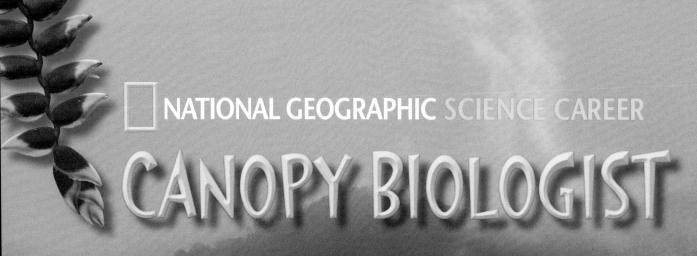

CANOPY BIOLOGIST

Meg Lowman

Bugs, leaves, and rope walkways—they are all part of the job for Meg Lowman. She works in the canopy ecosystem, among the uppermost rain forest branches.

NG Science: What do you do as a canopy biologist?

Meg Lowman: I act like a detective in the world's treetops. Sometimes I discover a new species. I specialize in insects that eat plants. A lot of my time is spent observing populations of beetles feeding on leaves. I try to learn which bug lives where, what it eats, and how it affects the health of trees. Then I try to figure out how everything interacts in the rain forest ecosystem to keep the entire planet healthy.

NG Science: What part of your job is most important to you?

Meg Lowman: My most important work has been to save rain forest ecosystems, one at a time, by building canopy walkways. Let's face it; forests are worth more alive than dead!

A dense rain forest covers about half of Belize, a country in Central America.

Lowman walks across a canopy raft to collect insect samples with her net.

Belize rain forest

GLOSSARY

C

community
(kuh-MYŪ-nuh-tē)

A community is made up of all the different populations that live and interact in an area. (p. 78)

condensation
(kon-den-SĀ-shun)

Condensation is the change from a gas to a liquid. (pp. 10, 52)

conservation
(kon-suhr-VĀ-shun)

Conservation is the protection and care of natural resources. (p. 30)

E

ecosystem (Ē-kō-sis-tum)

An ecosystem is all the living and non-living things in an area. (p. 76)

evaporation
(i-vap-uh-RĀ-shun)

Evaporation is the change from a liquid to a gas. (pp. 8, 50)

F

fossil fuel (FOS-ul FYŪ-ul)

A fossil fuel is a source of energy formed from plants or animals that lived millions of years ago. (p. 28)

H

humus (HYŪ-mus)

Humus is a part of soil made of decayed plants and animals. (p. 32)

M

matter (MA-ter)

Matter is anything that has mass and takes up space. (p. 4)

N

natural resources
(NA-chur-ul RĒ-sors-es)

Natural resources are living and non-living materials that are found on Earth that people use. (p. 26)

nonrenewable resources
(non-rē-NŪ-uh-bul RĒ-sors-es)

Nonrenewable resources cannot be replaced quickly enough to keep from running out. (p. 28)

O

orbit (ŌR-bit)

An orbit is the path Earth or another object takes as it revolves. (p. 58)

P

phase (FĀZ)

A phase is how the Moon appears from Earth. (p. 64)

plate (PLĀT)

A plate is a huge piece of Earth that moves slowly on a layer of very hot rock. (p. 40)

population
(pop-yū-LĀ-shun)

A population is all the individuals of a species that live in an area. (p. 78)

precipitation
(pri-sip-uh-TĀ-shun)

Precipitation is water that
falls from a cloud. (p. 54)

pulley (PUL-lē)

A pulley is a grooved wheel with
a cable or a rope running through
the groove. (p. 20)

R

renewable resources
(rē-NŪ-uh-bul RĒ-sors-es)

Renewable resources are
materials that are always being
replaced and will not run out.
(p. 26)

revolve (re-VAWLV)

To revolve is to travel around
another object. (p. 58)

rotate (RŌ-tāt)

To rotate is to spin around.
(p. 58)

runoff (RUN-awf)

Runoff is water that flows on
the surface of Earth. (p. 56)

S

soil (SOIL)

Soil is a layer of loose materials
on Earth's surface that is made
up of rock particles, humus, air,
and water. (p. 32)

states of matter
(STĀTS UV MA-ter)

States of matter are the forms
in which a material can exist.
(p. 4)

water cycle (WAH-tur SĪ-kul)

The water cycle is the movement
of water from Earth's surface to
the air and back again. (p. 50)

weather (WE-thur)

Weather is the state of the
atmosphere at a certain place
and time. (p. 46)

work (WERK)

Work is done when a force is
used to move an object over
a distance. (p. 16)

INDEX

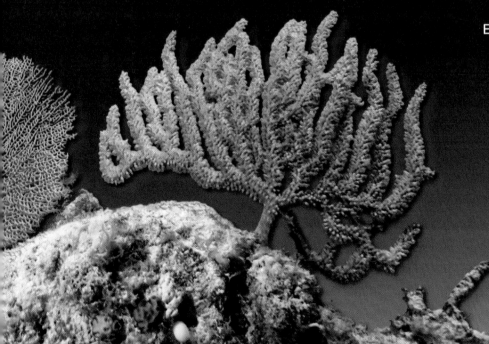

Photographs

PROGRAM CONSULTANTS

Randy Bell, Ph.D.
Associate Professor of Science Education,
University of Virginia, Charlottesville, Virginia
SCIENCE

Kathy Cabe Trundle, Ph.D.
Associate Professor of Early Childhood
Science Education,
The School of Teaching and Learning,
The Ohio State University, Columbus, Ohio
SCIENCE

Judith Sweeney Lederman, Ph.D.
Director of Teacher Education,
Associate Professor of Science Education,
Department of Mathematics and
Science Education,
Illinois Institute of Technology, Chicago, Illinois
SCIENCE

David W. Moore, Ph.D.
Professor of Education,
Mary Lou Fulton Teachers College,
Arizona State University, Tempe, Arizona
LITERACY

PROGRAM CONTRIBUTOR

Cathey Whitener, M.S. in Ed.
Science Specialist,
Marcella Intermediate School,
Aldine ISD, Houston, Texas
SCIENCE

Acknowledgments
Grateful acknowledgment is given to the authors, artists, photographers, museums, publishers, and agents for permission to reprint copyrighted material. Every effort has been made to secure the appropriate permission. If any omissions have been made or if corrections are required, please contact the Publisher.

STAAR is a trademark and/or federally registered trademark owned by the Texas Education Agency, and is used pursuant to license.

Photographic Credits
Front cover ©Darrell Gulin/Corbis.
(bkg) ©Siede Preis/Getty Images.
Back cover ©Darrell Gulin/Corbis.

Illustrator Credit
Precision Graphics.

Maps Credit
Mapping Specialists.

Acknowledgments and credits continued on page 97.

For permission to use material from this text or product,
submit all requests online at www.cengage.com/permissions

Further permissions questions can be emailed to permissionrequest@cengage.com

Visit National Geographic Learning online at www.NGSP.com

Visit our corporate website at www.cengage.com

Printed in the USA.
RR Donnelley, Jefferson City, MO

ISBN: 978-07362-93891

12 13 14 15 16 17 18 19 20 21

10 9 8 7 6 5 4 3 2 1